PRAISE for *When Men Bow Down.....*

Before you open this book, stop and say its title out loud. The repeated "en" of "When Men" and the repeated "ow" of "Bow Down" are not accidents (never mind that all three words that end in consonants end in "n"). The title is an alert that the poems you are about to read have been crafted by a poet who is paying attention, one who understands that *meaning* is not exhausted by *reference*. When such a poet writes, as R. Nemo Hill does, that "There is a path that leaves no man behind — / where no one's learning how to carry nothing," it is the No Man of Homer's Odysseus who is learning to carry Wallace Stevens' "nothing that is not there / And the nothing that is." Has learned that nothing is carried by timbre, and has chosen to carry it so.

H. L. Hix

R. Nemo Hill is a poet with a spark on his tongue, a mound of earth in his shoe, and some winged creature perched on his shoulder.

Wendy Videlock

From the shadows of grounded planes to the most intimate relations—mother and son, lover and lover—from "action / into stupefaction," the journeys of R. Nemo Hill are not just through places like Bali, Thailand, New York and San Francisco, but through awareness itself, which is always death-limned. These poems are essential artefacts of our psychological existence.

David Mason

What is R. Nemo Hill? 1) a philosopher, making the most of life as it is, not as it should be; 2) a traveler, who observes the world around him with an artist's eye and the people in it with respectful sympathy; 3) a red-blooded man, God bless him; 4) a gifted wordsmith who understands pacing, isn't afraid of complexity, and has a delicate touch with rhyme and meter;

5) an independent voice from outside the po-biz establishment, beholden to no one and indifferent to fads and trends; and above all, 6) a poet whose mind naturally rebels against neat little lists like this one. *Rose Kelleher*

R. Nemo Hill's beautifully ordered and disordered life is endlessly fascinating, and whenever the blizzards blow, I shall be able to escape to Bali. *Timothy Murphy*

WHEN MEN BOW DOWN

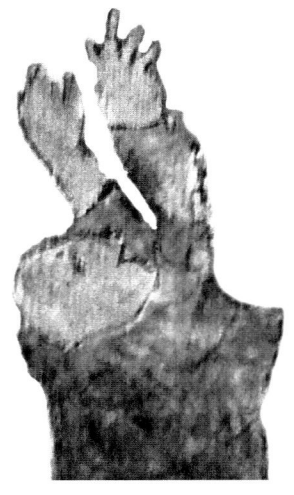

WHEN
MEN
BOW
DOWN

poems by

R. Nemo Hill

DOS MADRES
2012

DOS MADRES PRESS INC.
P.O.Box 294, Loveland, Ohio 45140
www.dosmadres.com   editor@dosmadres.com

Dos Madres is dedicated to the belief that the small press is essential to the vitality of contemporary literature as a carrier of the new voice, as well as the older, sometimes forgotten voices of the past. And in an ever more virtual world, to the creation of fine books pleasing to the eye and hand.

Dos Madres is named in honor of Vera Murphy and Libbie Hughes, the "Dos Madres" whose contributions have made this press possible.

Dos Madres Press, Inc. is an Ohio Not For Profit Corporation and a 501 (c) (3) qualified public charity. Contributions are tax deductible.

Executive Editor: Robert J. Murphy

Illustration & Book Design: Elizabeth H. Murphy
www.illusionstudios.net

Typset in Adobe Garamond Pro, Cambria & St. Columba
ISBN 978-1-933675-76-3
Library of Congress Control Number: 2012937277

First Edition

ACKNOWLEDGMENTS

The author would like to express his gratitude to the following publications in which certain of these poems previously appeared.

Looking Glass & Exile, *Smartish Pace*
A Bit Of Light, *Measure*
Still Water, *Quantuck Lane Press, The Countess of Flatbroke's Treasury*
Oasis & Bangkok Before Dawn & Soon, *Raintown Review*
Sonnet For Bill, *Poetry*
We Shall Entertain You, *Shit Creek Review*
Um Português, *14 by 14*
A Dog Barks In It & Heidegger's Traffic, *Big City Lit*
Silver Lining & To His Landlord, *Umbrella*
Invitation, *Tilt-a-Whirl*
Saint Junkie & Something Less, *Ganymede*
When Men Bow Down, *The Chimaera, Lilt*
Already, *Autumn Sky*
All That Is Needed, *First Things*
This Is The Hour & Sonnet To Green & Rain Can't Forget To Fall & Men And Darkness, *Soundzine*
In Distance, *American Arts Quarterly*
Jacaranda, *Think Journal*
'All upright things are bent and bowed by wind…', *Shot Glass Journal*
For An Aging Butterfly, *Anon*
The Mandarin Orange Tree, *Iambs & Trochees, The Countess of Flatbroke's Treasury*
Lovely Downcast Eye & A Lantern There, *Angle*

Cover: Painting by R. Nemo Hill
Author picture: Self-portrait by R. Nemo Hill includes photograph by Jeff Hill

Late in a season whose bright spark is you—.

for Julio

CONTENTS

…if one looked ahead, one saw dust and the backs of men's heads,
if one looked back, one saw the same dust and faces…

Anton Chekhov

I saw the open tavern-door flash on the dusk a ruddy glare,
And saw the King of Kings outcast reel brawling through the starlit air.
But yet He is the Prince of Peace of whom the ancient wisdom tells,
And by their silence men adore the lovely silence where He dwells.

George William Russell (A.E.)

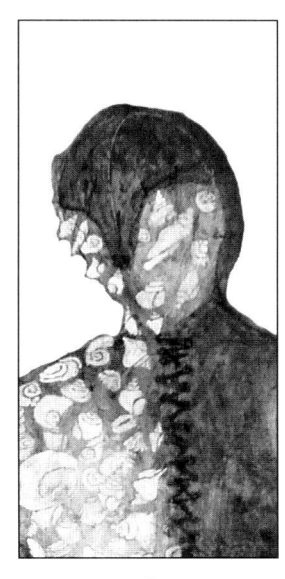

– 1 –

LOVELY
DOWNCAST
EYE

Looking Glass

I'm waiting for my flight. Time has slowed down.
It's stranded me before a wall of glass—
where, face to face, transparence and reflection
confound what is seen through with what glides past.
Outside it's pouring rain—a warm night's storm
has splashed the glass with drops, with waves of mist
through which I can discern the hulking forms
of grounded planes. Their shadowy shapes persist
beneath a veil of images less steadfast:
reflected movements and reflected light
cast ghost-like on the surface of dark glass
from inside, where it's cool and dry and bright;
the airport's solemn hubbub reproduced,
made weightless there—drained, flattened, and reduced.

I need not turn around at all to see them,
those moving by behind me constantly;
those passengers delayed, awaiting freedom,
whose shadows cross the glass impatiently.
They pace that lounge this mirror sets adrift,
past currency's exchange, through snack-bar's glow,
until the play of light and shadow shifts—
and they disappear—their luggage carts in tow.
And all the while the soundless storm is raging
in violent pantomime beyond thick glass,
while dulcet-toned bilingual voices paging
lost travelers, blend with the bland bombast
of piped in pop-tunes, and the journalese
of endless banks of pay-for-view tv's.

It's hard to know what's here and what is there,
what's in, what's out, what's on or through this glass,
what's real and what's a phantom—. Though I stare,
the solid state my eye presumes can't last.
The focus cannot hold. What then remains?
The only thing that seems real is this rain—
this rain I will believe in till the day
it washes every other thing away.
I see myself as well, in my glass place—
a tremulous mirage—but for my frown,
which seems the only part of my own face
this glass collage of weightlessness can't drown.
I watch my lips. They move without a sound.
They mouth four simple words: "Let it come down!"

(Changi Airport, Singapore—1998)

Pastel

I long to fade from action
into stupefaction,
slipping through the cracks
that restless fullness lacks.

I can no longer choose
between primary hues.
I crave complete collapse
into pastel gaps.

In torn mint and mallows,
by terracotta shallows,
where the gnat's lavender eye
kindles heat in a sigh;

on a vanishing palette, where black
is blind, and white is mute—
lay me on my back,
in brown mud and gray suit.

A Bit Of Light

(for my mother)

The night was moonless—dark as it can get
in this suburb where the porch-lights burn till dawn,
where the blue light of the neighbors' tv set
seeps through drawn curtains, silvering their lawn.
We both had fallen silent, lost in thought;
when suddenly she leapt up—"Look!" she cried—
and tottered round the garden till she'd caught
(with childlike skill) a single firefly.
"I haven't seen a firefly in years!"
she marveled at the lamp cupped in her palm.
"I thought that all of them had disappeared."
She held it closer, sheltering it from harm.
From between her fingers (clenched—but not too tight)
there leaked a blinking, greenish-yellow light.

A flash of inspiration swiftly followed.
"Where are you going?" I could scarce keep up.
"I'm looking for a jar, I want to show
your father—" "Are you sure? You'll wake him up."
"I'll put it in our room, beside the bed.
It's been so long since he has been outside.
I'll switch that goddamned tv off," she said.
"Go, tell him that I've brought him a surprise."
But halfway down the darkened hall she stopped,
and gazing through the glass, sighed with dismay.
"It won't light up," she said. "It knows it's trapped.
I guess the idea's silly anyway...
I'll let it go."
                    Outside, a single spark
escaped the jar and vanished in the dark.

(Massapequa, Long Island—2006)

4

A Lantern There

Ten tons of traffic overhead.
   The ground, the walls, the air, the sky,
   the hardness in each stranger's eye—
   all concrete. My left turns have led
   me far from showcase thoroughfares
   to streets eclipsed by the exhaust
   of the expressway thrust across
   the city's hidden quarters where
   once more I've chosen to be lost.

Rude mushrooms spring from constant murk.
   Beneath the belly of this beast
   a shadow-folk prepares its feast—
   a horde of vendors hard at work
   with wok and cleaver, propane, ice,
   in scrap-wood stalls: a tenement
   enfenced by pylons of cement
   which hoist aloft, past clouds of spice,
   this serpentine stone firmament.

Below, the ruptured urban crust.
   I'm forced to stare ahead and down,
   to navigate chaotic ground—
   till one descending curve, one gust
   of heavy heaven all but scrapes
   my skull.
              Compelled to twist my neck
   by some grim urban architect,
   my head is turned, my eyes escape
   from all they'd led me to expect.

I'm almost blinded by the glare.
   A squatting boy, with mortar and pestle,
   half-crushed beneath this concrete trestle—
   abject, and yet without despair,
   he's pounding peppers into paste,
   bright chilies, green and red, stripped bare
   of all that color can outstare;
   till they ignite, with fire as chaste
   as pole-starlight, a lantern there.

The traffic races by unseen.
   Head bowed to earth, a man nearby
   ignores the way it shakes the sky.
   His filthy hammock's strung between
   two power posts. He'll sit and play
   his solitary game of craps,
   with cards and dice and bottle-caps
   to guide him calmly on his way
   through life's incessant thunderclaps.

(Bangkok, Thailand—2007)

Not Far

For when the power of imparting joy
Is equal to the will, the human soul
  Requires no other heaven.
            — *Shelley, Queen Mab*

We gave him several precious ball point pens
(including one prize Parker T-Ball Jotter)
to supplement our coins, and make amends
for the exchange rate. As the day grew hotter
he chattered on, our ever-eager guide—
while we with sun-glazed eyes and sweat-soaked clothes
trudged on in mute obedience by his side,
numbed to a state of heat-induced repose.
An English teacher in a makeshift school
he hoped one day to do this!—that!—and more—!
Though young, he was quite clearly no one's fool.
In any other place he might go far.
But here? Unlikely. So it seemed to us.
Until our sense of just what distance was,
our map of what was near and what was far,
of what was great, too little, or enough—
was altered. We were circling the scarred
and earthquake-cracked and blasted rock, the rough
remains of what some long dead Buddhist king
had sworn would be the world's most wondrous pile
of stones—a monstrous stupa—that would bring
him endless merit, and be seen for miles—.
And yet it lay unfinished when he died,
all but the massive base, beyond which now
a flash of red cloth caught our young guide's eye,
cut short his tale of fallen kings and crowns,
and sent him scampering off through dust and stones
and what just might have been the old king's bones.

They stood some distance off, along the road—
two monks, mere boys—their novice robes of red
blurred by the waves of heat, their awkward load
of long blue plastic pipes deposited
beside them on the ground. His hand outstretched,
our guide approached, gave gifts, and then withdrew.
Against bright sun, we watched two silhouettes—
their small hands clasped and raised in gratitude.

"They run an errand for their monastery,
up in the hills," our guide explained. "Is it far?"
We eyed the pile of pipes. He smiled. "Don't worry.
They wait. Perhaps by dark...will come...the car."
They both were waving when we looked again.
"Yes," said our guide. "They thank you. For the pens."

(Mingun, Myanmar—2004)

Silver Lining

On the pavement just outside your door at dawn—
a double twist of dirty humped up nylon,
two suitcases, two stocking caps pulled down
towards facelessness, a cardboard sign hand-drawn:
'NO moNey and no tickET', a paper cup,
and a city poised to shake the still life up.

Your hands are in your pockets, jingling change.
Both sleepers shift and slightly rearrange
their sanctuary. Bits of skin appear,
one pale wrist caked with filth, a reddened ear.
And on one trembling eyelid—one thin line
of tarnished silver glinting through the grime.

There's warmth in that embrace, and even glamour.
An hour or more of city morning clamor
and you return to find them sitting there,
awake now—not quite smiling—as you stare
at the single bag of cookies that they share,
and the trace of henna lighting up her hair.

(Election Day, New York City—2008)

On Mahabandoola Road

Another face, another pair of hands,
another heap of something cheap for sale—
fried grasshoppers, or toothbrushes, or cans
of motor oil, or lard, or ginger-ale.
She's settled in the gutter by two tides:
by heat receding, and by darkness rising
and releasing chaos.
      Silently, she guides
me through this sea of brutish advertising
to her calm nocturne's shore. And leaves me there—.

Too hot to eat until the sun goes down
I've set out seeking sustenance, and share
the street with jostling hordes. This part of town
is prone to power failures—vendors lit
by single candles wedged in piles of fruit,
or edged in glare as passing car beams hit
them from behind. She does not stare, she's mute
and gestureless—the berries she would sell
seem no more red or sweet than those I've bought
from someone else; at least until that spell
her life so casually casts has caught
my own sense of proportion by surprise.

Two age-stained shallow baskets grace the ground
before her, full—they're lying side by side,
one scale, with balanced pans. The first is crowned,
piled high with ripened berries. In the other,
an infant sleeping with a fruit's quiescence.
She'll not return my gaze. She has, this mother,
no distance from her life—only presence.

(Yangon, Myanmar—2007)

Eggs And Strawberries

1

It's first a question of the weight of things,
for all things fall through space as well as time.
Can loss of gravity thus lend them wings,
these emptied vessels? Can it undermine
the heaviness inherent in design?
The famous bed of nails on which there rests
the sideshow swami is the paradigm
of all those bodies which, though manifest,
are somehow by their own concreteness undistressed.

Such carnival attractions may deceive.
And yet the evidence accumulates
that while the awful weight of living grieves
all those who bear the burden of brute fates—
yet, some things and some bodies make escapes
quite unexplained by normal means or measure.
A host of physical and mental states
from yogic discipline to simplest pleasure
bear buoyant witness to a loss that leads to treasure.

The white bloom balanced on the floating lotus.
The Buddha lightened of all hope and fear
who sits beneath a banyan tree unnoticed
and motionless for several thousand years.
The iconography is crystal clear.
Illusion some might call it—when we find
in clouds which drift above the earthly sphere
a lightness and a lithesomeness of mind
that leave the ball and chain of brain and skull behind.

2

The scene is one of traffic in descent;
a mountain track, a winding crowded road
which illustrates exactly what is meant
when it is said: each man bears his own load.
Ah, such a wealth of burdens is bestowed
by this red earth, red rich as rust or blood—
a heavy harvest, endless fount and flow,
a boundless cargo carried on a flood
of rattling flat-bed trucks all stained with dust or mud.

Piled high upon each over-laden truck—
the yielded fruits of a back-breaking toil;
whole fields of greens and onions, crudely plucked,
torn helter-skelter from their roots, their soil;
borne downhill in a convoy rudely royal.
Then round one curve (for brakes are known to fail)
one point of perfect stillness checks turmoil:
a smoking wreck—beached like a roadside whale—
spilled fallen melons littering its violent trail.

Right past the scene truck after truck rolls by.
There's little evidence of shock or grief.
Some twist their necks to see. Some close their eyes.
Some even heave a sigh, however brief,
of selfish yet forgivable relief.
They know their lives hang by a thread, a rope.
Just as at certain times of year, a leaf
must drop, they know men must abandon hope
as well as fear—in such a world, on such a slope.

The wreck itself has hardly passed from view
when suddenly, around the bend, appears
another point of stillness, moving through
the chaos of the roadway, calm and clear,
a carriage steered by a passive engineer—
a young boy, not quite smiling, traffic-tossed,
who sits not in the front but in the rear,
hands folded in his lap, legs lightly crossed,
head haloed by a smoky haze of truck exhaust.

He's perched in state, as if upon a throne—
a throne of such fragility he seems
to float above the toilsome stream, alone,
the weightless monarch of a waking dream.
And yet his journey is mundane, routine.
His mount's no bed of nails, no airy cloud,
no, the foundation stones of his regime
are hundreds of fresh eggs on which, somehow,
he sits with paranormal harmlessness endowed.

"Fresh eggs! Fresh eggs for sale!" he'll cry aloud
an hour later when the truck's descended
and stopped amidst the morning market's crowd.
Yet now, how to explain what has defended
the shells of these pale eggs on which, suspended,
this boy sits, into space so calmly staring—
that space in which all bodies are extended
and yet in which his own, despite this sharing,
displaces its own very substance with such daring?

3

Is it a question of the strength of things?
For all things must resist the crushing force,
the traffic of this world of weight—which clings
and presses down, which cramps and freights and thwarts.
These eggs themselves, bounced on their crashing course,
uncracked beneath the weight of this young Prince—
is mindfulness or mindlessness the source
of that uncanny act of balance whence
begins the end of all material violence?

Insanely sweet, though they look small and pale,
in shacks along this treacherous mountain road
there are fresh fragrant strawberries for sale—
their taste a grace upon poor men bestowed,
a meager fruit, a moment's vertigo!
What are these muscles, strengthened by collision?
These forms of might and mind? Mere dominoes
that topple, falling in complete submission,
undone by one sweet berry's sensual precision.

The smoking wreck is but an accident
of passing traffic, which may be illusion—
the elements of every incident
colliding in perpetual confusion.
Yet painful cuts and bruises, the contusions,
the wounds of mind and matter, all are based
on what may be but gravity's delusions—
grave weights by berries and eggshells erased
for poor men and young boys who yield to their embrace.

(Pyin Oo Lwin, Myanmar—2004)

14

Heidegger's Traffic

A man clattered and rang
on the rim of a glass
with a spoon
in the street
while I was starting out toward
sleep.

I wore his bell out walking
in my winding sheet.

Long lanes of all motion
open toward me, lead me,
and present to me the leavening
and the dread.
And unspool the string of no door closing
nor eye averting nor diverting
vision's stream of streaming,
vision's saying said.

Bell of sleep and wheel of waking
turning rings within
the corridor extended straight ahead.

While wheel of sleep and bell awakening
ringing turns within
where all appearing is

extended.

(Yogyakarta, Java—1991)

Exiles

The rain's been falling steadily since dawn.
By noon all trace of solid ground is gone.
The garden's flooded. Water on all sides.
My little porch alone rests high and dry—
a raft of rescue I'm obliged to share
with thousands of determined refugees
who scurry up the four legs of my chair
and sprint across the book closed on my knees.

I'd spent all morning gazing out—. I'd played
my role as the heroic castaway,
convinced I was alone. Till I looked down.
The horde of exiled ants runs circles round
the rim of my stained teacup, and my plate.
All hands on deck!—they cry. We cannot stay!
Our ark, though small, is all! The rest is groundless!
No anchor can take hold in what is boundless!

I feel the earth begin to tilt and sway—.
My porch, unmoored, is rocking on the waves—.

(Petulu, Bali—1997)

16

In Distance

And if we must carry further the offence of being born,
let us find, through the crowd, an opening toward the port
and the paths of unruled sea.

—St.-John Perse

1

I sailed for hours, no sign of life
on either shore: one lost in haze,
the nearer one a wide, bright white
expanse of sun scorched sand—ablaze.

They drifted slowly into focus
as I in turn went drifting by.
Eyes numb, at first I scarcely noticed,
but soon became preoccupied
and stared to ascertain the motives
of figures filling shallow pans
and hoisting them up on their heads—
pans laden with the very sands
through which they trudged, dispirited,
to empty them in shallow boats
they'd beached along the burning strand.
Sand everywhere, on land, afloat,
a desert and a sea of sand—
on fire in the sun. It seemed
proverbial absurdity
to shift it from point a to b.

And drifting closer I could see
other figures, drunkenly
chasing one another round
in circles—like mad circus clowns:
pigs and naked children playing
foolish games, and yet obeying

laws of motion as austere
as those by labor engineered—.
All blurring as they disappeared
behind me—. All reduced to bits,
to voiceless specks, confetti drifting,
running, laughing, hauling, lifting—
with pitiful deliberateness.

2

With one hand raised against the glare
that all but veiled the distant shore,
I watched four upright figures there—
four silhouettes that seemed no more
than fenceposts hammered, senseless, in
the mud along this river's bank.
Four lifeless things.
                                        Yet noticing
how gaps between them grew, then shrank,
(sans locomotive evidence)
the only thing that moved, I sensed,
was air itself—the breach between—

space seemed the only living being.

While men or women (who could say
the difference from far away?)
were incidental measurements,
a system of brute calibration,
mere marks revealing the extent
of one invisibly immense
and omniversal respiration.

3

And as with figures, so with voices—
cries from far afield, ashore—.
Stripped of sense, reduced to noises,
prattler soon turns troubadour.
Drifting far from care-worn sources,
bleached of intent and design,
distance lends all man's discourses
a music, born of bare resources,
enigmatically benign.

Till human "hey" and "howdy-do,"
the tête-à-tête of me and you
(the whole terrestrial interview)
dissolves like birdsong in the trees
or water lapping tirelessly
at river's edge, beyond the reach
of the mundane excuse for speech.

4

Is it time then for one man,
one weary traveler—to land,
to disembark?
                    Though the plateau
be post-apocalyptically
unpeopled; though it throb and glow
with terminal toxicity
and chemical abandon; though
fires scour the distance, raging...
its emptiness will yet engage him.
He will not dwell upon the fallen.
He would not come were they to call him.

Red dusts invade. Dead cows and flies.
Charred slopes where heaps of metal rise
like altars craving sacrifice.
And cruel winds that sweep away
the plastic cup, the rusted ring,
the bulb that lit the cabaret,
the oar whose constant paddling
and horse whose painful saddling
had marred the solitary way

that blue-green moonlight has of weaving
the dreams of one who's always leaving:
the exile.
             Hush——. He's home at last——.
His vision fading, growing faint,
his figure scars the rising distance
like a moving daub of paint.

(Ayeyarwady River, Myanmar—2007)

Still Waters

The flame's gone out.
It casts no light.
I cast myself
Into the night.
Frail boat I sink
Into the sea.
Still water's dark.
Still water's deep.

Asleep I fall.
Asleep I rise.
The cradle tips.
The darkness sighs.
A tumbling child
Wakes in my eyes.
Still water flows.
Still water flies.

And caught beneath
The wing of sleep
I cling
To nothing
Rising.

Reading Aloud To The Corpses Of My Parents

The speed of light slows to a crawl—.
It falters—. Then it grabs a hold
of wheelchair chrome, of wedding gold—.
They're barely burnished. That is all
the light I have to read by.

Half filled glasses in their hands
are tipping—almost spilling. Lapse
and loss have given birth to gaps
I need to fill. My voice expands
the silence it is freed by.

"Your father wants to hear you read—
from your own book." So I brewed tea.
And gladly silenced the tv.
Their eyes closed almost instantly
the moment I'd begun.

Yet if I stop, they soon protest,
they're wide awake with loving smiles—
a Pharaoh and his Queen beguiled
by prospects of eternal rest:
"Just read us chapter one."

It can't be true my book's that boring.
Her dropped jaw. His tilted head.
They cannot possibly be dead,
I tell myself, I hear them snoring.
Such peace, I can't deny them.

The force of breath descends to drift—.
It fades—. Then steadies to a wheeze.
And in that all but failing breeze
two sails too briefly sigh, and lift
a voice to lullaby them.

(Massapequa, Long Island—2008)

For An Aging Butterfly

Two wings—. One's perfect yellow diamonds scattered
across the sapphire dust of its blue membrane.
The other's naked gray transparence tattered,
a wasted autumn leaf's stained cellophane.
A mismatched pair, inhibitors of flight—
their daring lack of symmetry has stranded
this broken butterfly. And yet despite
its crippled state—the leaf on which it's landed
provides sufficient turf to promenade
like some weak-ankled, blue-haired matriarch
insisting on her jeweled, high-heeled facade
while strolling on a spring day through the park.
Sunlight reveals caked powder on her face.
She limps with genteel orthopedic grace.

(Petulu, Bali—1996 / Gramercy Park, New York City—2006)

Walking in a Capital City on the Day After Rain, 1884

What is the name of this provincial street?
A threadbare Chopin waltz for metronome
and fugitive polite piano leaks
out through the solid curtains of each home.

Now plane trees. And a passing tram. I light
a cold cigar. In open coach, quick glimpse:
two ladies wearing black, stiff-backed, contrite,
put on their gloves. A little girl who limps

is clutching at an orange. In an alley
a housemaid's beating clouds of dust, pale blue,
from woolen rugs. Let's walk more quickly, shall we?—
before it settles on our polished shoes.

This mood of melancholy's mass-produced
until it's swallowed by monotony.
I'm looking at the women's faces, trying to
perceive the everydayness of their destiny.

And all the windows are like sightless eyes.
One can imagine: the dining room's ennui
of burnished spoons; the perfect compromise
of sálon; the immutability

of master bedrooms. A canary, caged,
is silent at one window; more content,
at another, a young man's raised the shades—
he's smiling, as if he's just paid his rent.

Two nurses meet and stop to chat awhile.
Their infant charges, during this forced pause,

look over stiff starched shoulders—both beguiled
by windblown leaves and several stray dogs.

(after Jules Laforgue—Notebook, 1884-5)

Bangkok Before Dawn

Through my double pane of hotel glass
there's only one sound dull enough to pass:
the traffic river's roar ten stories down,
in which the first few songs of birds will drown.

There's light—. A burning blur of distant car-parks,
an acid yellow glare, a nuclear hum.
And lit like square, cold, artificial sparks
in concrete slabs—blank windows, deaf and dumb.

The traffic song drones on. I cease to listen.
Into a shallow sky of threadbare brown
I stare out from my air-tight air-con prison—
convinced for this brief hour: there is no ground.

There is no earth to grasp. No star for wishing.
And this ochre moon? It's full of all that's missing—
a round and empty television screen
on which (all broadcast ended) nothing's seen.

(Pinnacle Hotel—2004)

Soon

The room shrank when I entered. It collapsed
around me until all that it could hold
were two old men reduced to weathered scraps,
and one low country crone—her voice made bold

by years of afternoons spent in that gap
between their two gray burgers and her glass
of weak iced tea. And now look what the map
had dragged in from the road which ran right past

this minor luncheonette that closed at four—
anticipating dusk. In her bent spoon,
she weighed each word while staring at the door.
"I think," she said, "the Lord will come back soon."

An awful silence. Followed by the hiss
of hot grease on the grill. Then that too died
as average sibyl challenged the abyss:
"God said he would, and God has never lied."

A cup of styro too damn hot to hold
preoccupied me lest I trip, or spill
and burn—before I'd crossed the final threshold
of one small world grown prematurely still.

"The thing is—. His idea of soon, and ours,
they're not the same," one scrap of man remarked
impassively. I summoned all my powers
of flight and, clutching coffee, disembarked

from one ark to another—one refilled
with just-pumped gas. My steaming coffee proved
a thin and sour brew. Yet as I swilled
its tastelessness, it gradually removed

that drowsy veil that settles on the senses
of one who has been driving for too long
through vacant hills, scarred by unmended fences—
hills graced by barns and houses far too strong

to crumble, though abandoned to each season.
Bleached gray by sun and rain, walls warped and tilting,
just waiting to give way—each yet finds reason
to stand alone, perpetually wilting.

(Andes, New York—2010)

Lovely Downcast Eye

How, lovely downcast eye, resist the color of the ground?
How not absorb that dust, as resolute in hue as stone,
that gathers, tired and gray, wherever distant roads are found
returning with the chastened gaze that strayed beyond the bone,
beyond the gristle, beam and bracket, tooth and nail and groan?
And how, poor tired eye, resist stern architecture's round
of haul and hoist and harness—its weights and pulleys, aching, straining.
And all to lift what weightlessness? To carve from hush what sound
but this—our labored breathing, and our anguished sighs complaining
of sweet dreams smothered by life's constant building and explaining.
Hard then, our hardened vision mounts, our hard cathedrals rise.
As heroes then, we throw our muddy anchors to the skies.

But now—.
        If I could write about the color of the ground
as if it were a bowl of roses where I gently sway,
one fawn-flesh colored sail amidst countless crimson others, bound
by distant curve, thin-pressed where dew meets deep below— I'd say:
Transform this hard Foundation Stone! And in the corner lay
what coils, what undulates, first petal of the Red Real Church
that blossoms not quite where we stand and not quite where we search.

Oasis

From time to time I lost sight of the beast.
He'd overtake me, vanish down the road—
the crooked trail of dark wet prints he'd leave
fading on the pavement as I followed,
evaporating in the noonday sun.
And then when I assumed I was alone,
he'd reappear from somewhere just behind me
and pass me once again, quite unconcerned,
as if he knew exactly where he'd find me.
He never looked at me, he never turned
around to bark, or growl—he made no sound—
tongue lolling, water dripping from his fur,
wet paw prints painted freshly on the ground.

We were the only two crazed creatures walking.
And from their shaded perches I could sense
the local citizenry gently stalking,
with lazy eyes, these dangerous innocents:
fool foreigners and dogs who brave the heat
to spend the midday hours out on their feet.
But I knew well the violence of this sun.
I rather liked the fever it induced;
the shimmer it lent each phenomenon;
the flood of perspiration it set loose;
the lightness of the head, the heavy eye;
but most of all that sense of solitude
on empty roads where no one else passed by.

Perhaps the fickle beast did not exist—.
Perhaps it was a heat hallucination?
I had almost convinced myself of this
when, once, the apparition kept me waiting

for far too long. I stopped. Where had he gone?
I gazed with shaded eyes in each direction.
Then glanced, by chance, down to the unseen gutter
that hemmed the steep embankment by the road:
a rank canal of shallow, greasy water
so clogged with rotting trash it scarcely flowed.
A filthy dog's oasis. And there he lay.
I looked back once to see if he would follow.
And then went on my solitary way.

(Jalan Tegallalang, Bali—1997)

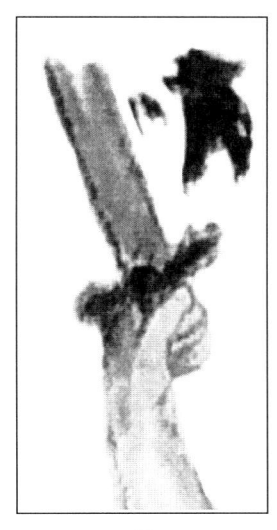

– 2 –

THE
SONS OF HECUBA
PRESENT
THEIR WOUNDS

The Arborist

Handshake unsolicited, disarmingly direct,
his quick self-sketch delivered up point-blank—

sculptor, surgeon, arborist, an aerial architect,
a master of 'precision cuts'. We drank

to 80 feet above the earth, suspended by a rope
stretched tight as his taut tales. He pointed down—.

Trimming trees was treacherous, but precious few could cope
with felling them in peopled parts of town.

Oaks had earned his deep respect. Old oaks were sacrosanct.
I hymned those standing on my mother's lawn—

lonely titans towering, they'd long since been outflanked
by hedge-rowed miles of flat suburban spawn.

Intimacy thus achieved, I'd earned another beer
and, on my shoulder, one strong callused hand,

brashly tender, terrified, and brutally sincere—
a boastful boy's touch, hidden in a man.

Further confidences followed, chiefly this admission:
he hoped one day to 'certify' his climb—.

True tree surgeons learned to cut with renegade precision,
but bureaucrats had made their art a crime.

Stymied by injustices, he clawed at his cold beer,
splay-fingered, with a flat yet agile thumb.

A cigarette, abruptly cadged, appeared behind one ear
as he drifted off, our conversation done.

(The Hole In The Wall Bar, San Francisco—2008)

Saint Junkie

From far away—a single tuft of dark green tangled hair,
a savage cowlick sprung from terraced houses neatly combed.
I climb the hill, and stop before a flight of concrete stairs
to catch my breath; then disappear into the trees, alone.

The forest's windward side is twisted by the constant blast,
its rugged slopes deserted save for those who seek the sea—
which beckons from brute distance when this steep ascending path
curves round, emerging from the thicket unexpectedly.

Wind at my back, sea heavy on my shoulder, I approach
the leeward wood—. Here men desire things more close to hand.
Here it is still, and hot. And solitary figures float
in silence through a grotto of gnarled branches, sun, and sand.

From far away—a public park, primeval.
From deep within—a hive, where paths converge.
They cross and loop, they mount, then tumble,
wracked by roots they crack and crumble
to sandy track or windy funnel.
They crest and then are once more re-submerged.

The rhythmic motion of his pale hand beating from behind
a wall of briar & bramble—that's what first attracts my eye.
It sends me creeping closer round his shelter till I find
the entranceway that frames the boy: with pants dropped to mid-thigh,

with white shirt, buttoned to the neck, stained red by drops of wine,
and fingers scarred by scabs his shattered nerves will not let heal.
His jet black greasy curls catch one bright ray of light and shine.
He's desperate for cash, I'm sure, yet too bemused to steal.

Poor young junkie, is he twenty? I should judge, and scold.
And yet as I stand frozen on the threshold of his hovel,
he meets my gaze in silence—with eyes of silver-gray and gold
that make me drop down recklessly upon my knees, and grovel.

Eyes lit from far away. Eyes wordless, pleading.
Their colors won't survive intact much longer—.
Silver flash will soon retreat,
stunned to steel. The burning heat
of gold will burn to brown defeat.
Will loss of luster prove him older, stronger?

Head propped up at an angle by a pile of broken stone,
he's stretched out on his back, on a torn blanket in the dirt;
resting like an obscene mummy in a catacomb,
one pale hand pressed between his thighs. He cannot say a word—.

He's struggling to express himself, and yet his bloodstream racing
in contrary directions leaves him eloquent—but mute.
A dozen jagged shards of broken mirror that he's placed in
sight, assure him a derangement nearly absolute.

Kaleidoscope? Or system of surveillance? Worse, perhaps—.
Perhaps he'll slit my throat, I think, as I reach out one hand;
then notice how he studies, in his shattered looking glass,
those shadows cast upon the branches by each passing man.

From outside—an illicit, sordid meeting.
From deep within—a refuge, strangely pure.
That pale hand in the dim light beating
like a wounded dove, entreating
exit?—entrance? Here, between them,
in this hut: one briefly opened door.

(Buena Vista Park, San Francisco—2005)

When Men Bow Down

When men bow down to sip their drinks
their all-night neon halos tip,
casting shadows as they slip
across pale brows that slowly sink
and drown together, drip by drip,
what each man feels, what each man thinks,
when men bow down to sip their drinks.

When men bow down to sip their drinks
in dimmed down day or midnight's glare,
in common rows or solitaire,
in a silence startled by the clink
of ice on glass—as if in prayer,
their eyes close and their focus shrinks
when men bow down to sip their drinks.

When men bow down to sip their drinks
with shoulders hunched, with jaws grown slack—
draped across each turned, bent back
the world's abandoned at the brink
of their immobile zodiac,
their cloud of mingled breath which stinks
as men bow down to sip their drinks.

When men bow down to sip their drinks
the rhythmic round of hand to lip
grows metronomic, each man's grip
preserves his final failing link
to time—. Of passing moments stripped,
the present stares, the future blinks,
when men bow down to sip their drinks.

(Dick's Bar, 1992-2007—New York City)

The Sons Of Hecuba Present Their Wounds

Hear Mother, how the arrow–shaft passed straight through both my hands—
The more my blood poured down the reins, the more the horses ran.

Oh Mother, one swift spear emerged between my shoulder blades—
And through the hole punched in my lungs, the breath fell in cascades.

My arm was severed, Mother, see? Blood soaked the earth like rain—
Drained dry, the wound, a gaping mouth, is all that now remains.

Up through the groin the spear passed, till my liver felt its sting—
I tore it, Mother, from my flesh. Blood gushed as from a spring.

I saw the bow stretched taut, O Mother, saw the arrow fly—
My brow pierced, I saw red, as steaming blood submerged my eyes.

Hear Mother, how no shield could halt the savage spear's blood lust—
It tore my heart out through the ribs and flung it into dust.

O Mother, even as I knelt and pleaded for my life—
I choked upon the blood that burned my throat and bathed the knife.

The sword, O Mother, crashed so hard, I could no longer stand—
So on my knees I watched my blood flow through my outstretched hands.

From right to left the sword, O Mother, opened up my breast—
My heart lay gasping like an infant slaughtered in its nest.

I fell, O Mother, to the ground, sword lodged deep in my side—
And there I lay until its thirst for blood was satisfied.

Straight through the neck, the spear, O Mother, pinned me to the ground —
I screamed: a bloody foam boiled from my mouth without a sound.

See Mother, how, legs broken, I lay on the battlefield—
No bone uncracked by horse's hoof, uncrushed by chariot's wheel.

One sword stroke sliced the flesh; the second, Mother, cleft the bone—
I heard the muscle tear before my head dropped like a stone.

The sharpened point, O Mother, pressed against, then through my cheek—
Its thrust unchecked although I clenched the blade between my teeth.

The blade, O Mother, razor sharp, slit smoothly through my wrist—
My pulse erupted in the air above my severed fist.

O Mother, know my armor failed, its bronze all forged in vain—
My breastplate pierced, my helmet sheltered only cries of pain.

Know Mother, to a single spear both horse and rider fell—
And in a ditch we bled as one, drenched in each other's hell.

The blow, O Mother, smashed the jaw; my teeth were all torn out—
My tongue exploded in a jet of blood inside my mouth.

I screamed out when the arrow stabbed the tender belly's flesh—
Against the wound, O Mother, see my bloodied fingers pressed.

For A Gardener

His right hip has a swivel to it—very slight—
　　Yet just enough to misalign the knee;
And then, in turn, to twist the ankle, so the foot
　　Can never quite fall flat upon the ground.
 While working—his long, mud-stained trousers may conceal
　　The skewed mechanics of each step he takes;
But in idle hours, torn shorts reveal the flaw
　　That haunts all his attempts at forward motion.
Where others proceed swiftly, moving straight ahead—
　　His pace is somewhat slower, and it slants—
Its angle hardly crippling, but oblique enough
　　To mark him out as he who hesitates,
As he who draws back calmly from the starting line
　　Because he's chosen not to run this race.

Now, this is not a place where profit's devil waits
　　At every lonely crossroads, striking deals:
I'll give you this for that—or that for only this—.
　　Ambition drives a subtler bargain here.
Yet even so his quiet modesty is striking,
　　His limp a humble, humanizing anchor
That moors him resolutely to his earth's green crust.
　　 His patience blending with his habitat,
His fate's the triumph of a gentler evolution:
　　I'm just a gardener. No more than that.

The garden path is laid out in a sort of circle
　　With no beginning—thus without an end.
And every afternoon at half past four o'clock,
　　(Alerted by the angle of the sun)
He sweeps this endless path as planned, with true devotion,
　　Same time, same place, same slow and steady rhythm—

The hand that grips the bamboo broom, in constant motion,
   His free hand resting, still, behind his back.
And every afternoon I hear him from my porch,
   And look up from my reading just in time
To watch the leaves drop lightly to the clean-swept path
   Behind him, moments after he's passed by—
To make it clear, with each determined step he's taking,
   How little progress he indeed is making.

(Petulu, Bali—2004)

Sonnet For Bill

Even reaching for a bourbon or a beer
your hands seemed always gracefully composed.
Their elegance intact, though more severe,
all that they've held, or wrestled with, still shows—
although they reach for nothing now. They lie
like orchids, dropped upon the white sheet stretched
across your ribs, your chest—which I watch rise
and fall—a small, pale pine cone filled with breath.

Forgive me now if face to face with death
I turn to paint a portrait more discreet:
a single glass of warm milk that's been left
to cool beside a window. In the street
outside, long shadows of late afternoon
are gathering and entering your room.

(New York City—2006)

45

Rain Can't Forget To Fall

The air so heavy, but this rain so light
and pressureless. Can rain forget to fall?
The pavement, dull. This rain so fine, so bright,
invisible. Scant trace of it at all
but for this sound that seems to steal both weight
and voice from all things metal, concrete, glass—
this distant damp dust hush content to wait
till rigid things, grown lush, bow like wet grass.

A dragon tattooed on his single leg,
soaked shirt stuck to thin shoulders, crutch hand swollen,
too busy struggling forward now to beg—
one man bears all those burdens light rain's stolen.
For at the moment he is overtaken,
its empty whispering abruptly ceases—
as the weight of all brute things is re-awakened
in these torrents splintered wood on stone releases.

Scant trace remains of silence now at all.
Rain's found its voice. Rain can't forget to fall.

(Bangkok, Thailand—2008)

46

To His Landlord

(Julius Eastman, 1940-1990)

Perhaps you don't remember him at all.
Such two-bit low-life losers come and go.
You used to ambush him out in the hall
demanding your back rent. He'd answer slow
and easy, quoting scripture with a sigh:
The Camel and The Needle's Eye. Yeah—. Sure—.
The one with all the cats, the skinny black guy
in leather pants who never locked his door.
You blamed it then on drugs and alcohol.
But I guess you don't remember now at all.
Nah. I really can't expect you to recall.

But even if you did—how could you know
that in that doorless closet piled with trash
a hibernating Grail lay lost below
the dirty clothes and cat shit: a sacred cache
of scores, handwritten scores—which music scholars
are reconstructing now from rare cassettes,
transcribing notes by ear. It seemed mere squalor,
the day the Marshals hauled it out and set
the whole mess on the curb. Sad episode.
Such no-count nameless losers come, then go.
There really was no way that you could know.

And yet I can't help wondering: might you care?
It's been what? Twenty years? And still I see you,
out bicycling in skin tight Lycra-wear.
You're keeping fit. That's smart. You smile more too.
I'd like to tell you just what was inside
those plastic bags dragged from apartment four.
I want to say: he's fabled now, that guy

who never paid his rent or locked his door.
You look right through me as if I'm not there.
And even if I told you—could you care?
I almost spoke today. But didn't dare.

(New York City—2007)

The Pedicure

From the walker to the diaper (just in case)
to the low car door that almost guillotines him—
I reckon it too high a price he pays
to have ten toenails cut.
                                  "You haven't seen them!
They're fossilized, inch-thick—they get infected."
Yet it seems that modern medicine's perfected
the art—round trip, quick clip, just half an hour—
then twice that long to trundle him inside.
"So, how'd it go?"
                            "It hurt. But he's no coward."
I ask him then if he enjoyed the ride.
No answer.
              "And it didn't cost a dime.
The nurse said he could come back any time."

I glance at him—the beneficiary
as well as the long since indifferent broker
of health insurance plans that I can see
concern him far less now than tv poker.
"If not, she said to try Vicks VapoRub…"
"You're kidding!"
                          "It'll soften them right up."
A menthol phantom from my childhood grows,
dissolves across my chest.
                   "Or Listerine.
She said we only had to soak his toes…"
"In mouthwash?"
                The nostalgic childhood scene
gives way at once to a tableau more ruthless.
I see myself years hence, bald, toothless,
marooned before a wide screen flat tv—
my Cool Mint foot-bath life's last luxury.

(Massapequa, Long Island—2007)

49

Men Like These

A scrap of greasy paper, flecked with rice,
lies crumpled on the pavement in between them.
Their meager midday meal's been shared (its price
sometimes a full day's labor) and the men
lie still now, stretched out on their backs, content
on this hard dusty bed of bare cement.

The shop's abandoned, or perhaps just closed
to beat the awful heat this time of day.
The two lean barefoot traveling salesmen doze,
collapsed beside each other in its shade.
Its porch, one sheet of warped and rusted tin,
grants rude though peaceful shelter to these men
who trudge for miles along scorched rutted roads,
their shoulders bent beneath preposterous loads—

from blocks of ice to shackled ducks and roosters;
from plastic children's toys to towering stacks
of hand-made wooden chairs, or monstrous clusters
of coconuts; from aphrodisiacs
and cures for lice, to popsicles, and pencils,
and other less decipherable utensils.

A hierarchy of some sort does prevail—
first motored carts whose musical refrains,
mechanically rigged, solicit sales;
then cyclists with horns or bells to gain
attention more abruptly for their wares;
next those who hitchhike round to village fairs
and markets; and on down to men like these—
who only walk—slow, steady, silently.

Beneath that porch, whose shadows almost hide them,
they sleep now in their quiet concrete pasture.
Yet burdens laid down casually beside them
seem far more restless than their restful masters:
two bamboo barbells balanced at both ends
with dangling fruits of singular transparence.

Strange artificial fruits—these prove to be
bouquets of plastic bags, filled up with water,
then knotted and suspended carefully
like ripe grapes, or trussed animals for slaughter.
They're drinking water salesmen! one decides—.
Until a flash of orange sparks provides
swift proof that circling endlessly within
each liquid satchel—three bright goldfish swim.

(Ubud, Bali—1997)

We Shall Entertain You

I remember the night preceding this dangerous liaison. Before me I saw a tomb.
I heard a glowworm huge as a house say to me: "I shall entertain you . . ."
                                        —*Le Comte de Lautréamont*

The pulpit was a spring-sprung cot that reeked
of all the tortured fluids that had leaked
from raving lunatics, their liquid heavings.
The church—a tabernacle of their foulest grievings,
the Quatrième Fiévreux, Fourth Fever Ward
of Val-de-Grace—its back-house corridor—
nocturnal temple of a splinter sect of mental science,
pews padlocked to insure strict congregational compliance.

The liturgy? Les Chants de Maldoror,
the psalms of the demented troubadour
declaimed each long dark night, till dawn exposed
young poets cloaked in drab night-watchmen's clothes—
volunteers for late shifts others shunned.
"André! Louis! Enough! The doctors come!"
Surrealists administering nightmares to the damned,
they'd hide their text, salute, and leave—as iron doors were slammed.

Oh, how they thrilled the night that cry arose!
In crippled chorus from behind the rows
of bolted doors they heard the inmates shriek:
"You're crazy—!"
                        "Ahh, the ultimate critique,
one madman to another!" howled André,
reciting scripture now with doubled rage—
while outside the locked ward, the wail of sirens and the din
of a cruel World War's bursts of cannonfire were closing in.

(Paris—Spring, 1918)
(after Mark Polizzotti)

52

Angelology

(for my father)

Not gilded. Rather trimmed with polished chrome,
reflecting tepid antiseptic light.
And not on wings, but wheels—whose squeaking metronomes
abrade the edges of each moment's flight.

Not hovering, no. Not quiet. Not alone.
But trumpeted by ten translucent tubes
that calculate the breathing—while a sterile drone
of bleeps and drips ticks off what's left to lose.

Then over my stooped shoulder as I sigh
and drop my eyes—a single raven wave
swoops through the room. By darkness dignified,
suddenly my timid prayers grow brave:

Pale scrubbed mechanics, hurrying to and fro—
this bedside shadow can't be bleached. Now let him go.

(Long Island—2007)

Still Life With Weightless Gift

(for Paco)

When we wish will all arrive transparently
                              —Robert Desnos

No glimmer yet of sun on the horizon—
the first cock still uncrowed, a bug-eyed gecko
still hunting moths beneath dark dew-thatched eaves.
My cup of steaming tea is but a shadow,
just one of many, on the table—near
a shallow bowl of passion fruit, a melon,
a candle stub, a cucumber, a book,
an empty tube of strong insect repellent.

No trace now of that hollow bamboo seahorse
set with broken glass, reflecting light,
hovering, suspended, motionless
in the glittering water of my dream last night—.
In a rundown local woodshop yesterday
I'd priced a seahorse, carved from ebony,
and had considered buying it for a friend
who was tattooed with one just recently.

I came home empty-handed. I still am.
And yet a gift in dream or reverie,
where purchase is beside the point, may be
of far more value—freed entirely
from its box and paper wrapper, from its baggage
of counted coin, its ribbon and its bow,
and its delivery tax.
                              A weightless message—
the imprint of one's head upon the pillow,
the only material stamp one has to show.

(Petulu, Bali—1996)

54

Something Less

Dark-haired, dark-eyed, dark-skinned, and paper-thin—
each wrist's a restless ballerina bird
in nervous flit around a table ringed
with decadent old Frenchmen undeterred
by dog-eared menus. "—Shall we order?"

Cuisine Hotel Malaysia advertises
familiar fare on my first jet-lagged night,
the usual blend of chili pastes and spices—
as well as something extra: this dark sprite
whose eyes meet mine, here, at the border

of age and youth, where stillness counters flux.
Why does he stare—? Is he so mercenary
he'd add my own small change to those big bucks
he's prancing for? Or is he merely weary,
seeking rescue? No. —It's something less.

The coyness in his dance about the room
is absent from his gaze. I feel relieved,
reduced to landscape.
                        Dark, yet without gloom—
unblinking, and yet blank—his eyes receive,
and yet give nothing back. They acquiesce

with animal indifference. My eyes
relax as well. I do not look away.
Pressed, pressureless, together—we de-vivify
a world whose sordid sentient shadowplay
continues all around us. Quite unheeded

amidst all these transactions of desire
by which it's ambushed, this numbed contact glows—
a moment deepened by cold shallow fire;
a gem, unfaceted, whose color barely shows,
reflecting little light—no more than needed.

(Bangkok, Thailand—2006)

Men and Darkness

As evening entered
          long storms were ending.
Reduced to a rumbling
            ruined by distance,
thunder grew thinner,
             threatening others.
Hemingway's hoisted
          his gun to his head,
he's fired, and fallen.
           The finished book
lies in my lap,
        listing toward shadow
as a drenched day
          draws to a close
with the power and pressure
             of that final page.
He's tripped the trigger
          just in time
for the lamps are lit
         a moment later.
My bare feet lifted
        from the flooded porch,
legs bent beneath me
         in my bamboo chair,
I've read what remains
          of the written record
of the self-slain slayer
        of so many beasts.
But I'm barely able
        by this low watt bulb
to see myself now,
        much less some other.

(13 February, 1999—Petulu, Bali)

Um Português

(for Paulo)

That phone line is so old I rarely answer.
Retrieving messages is just routine:
my credit score, pitched sales, the march for cancer,
cheap satellite tv—a general theme.
I've been away. Press play, m-hmm, delete...
I'm caught off-guard—and smiling, raise my head.
I recognize your accent instantly
and yet it isn't you. It says: you're dead.

The winter fog that rolled in from the coast
would swallow up that old stone house, and hold me
for days on end, alone. That haunts me most.
"You've such respect for silence—" you once told me,
"—you leave the room, and gently close the door."
The ghost in my machine says nothing more.

(February—2008)

This Is The Hour

The herons turn towards home, their course unfailing.
Below them, miles of earth grow dim and still—
for the wind has fallen, and the light is trailing
not far behind—.
                         Though hardly visible
the switched-on garden lamps already wait
for moths who'll spin for them bewildered halos;
as the blue of the sky darkens to wet slate,
and the first few bats swoop through the open windows.

This is the hour when a falling leaf or flower
drops straight down to the ground with a light, lost tap.
This is the hour when the body cedes its power
to those shadows it is now too weak to cast.

And the mist—if it rises—
and the dark—as it falls—
are alive, and alert,
each a potent companion

for any man who finds himself alone.

(Petulu, Bali—1997)

– 3 –

THE
BRIGHT
STINKING

Dawn Journal

In the east—dull white, and an even paler blue
give way to strata of unripening peach—
and then to one thin thread of lime drawn through
those distant palms the light has not yet found the strength to reach.

The old cock in the hutch beyond the hedge
is cackling now with ritualized emotion—
he too has noticed dawn's painterly touch
and raises harsh Hosannas! of fanatical devotion.

Gray shadows of gray cats glide through gray leaves.
The fish rise from the pond's depths to its borders
to nibble at half-light. How silently
their skittery kisses stir the brightening skin of murky water.

Impatient for the psalm's refrain to pass
to them—birds wait. But crickets, not yet through,
resist surrender, hidden in wet grass—
and the lawn continues humming, drenched in sonic waves of dew.

One final fat mosquito buzzes past.
One swift clap of my hands disturbs the calm
of my own heartbeat. Yet my coup-de-grace
yields no tell-tale spot of blood, but only stinging palms.

(Petulu, Bali—2005)

Sonnet To Green

Astounding pale green garden—6 a.m.—
it glistens after last night's steady rain.
Each leaf's a faint yet brilliantly green gem
by moisture set translucently aflame;
as if the sun were rising from within
each tissue—not just spreading like a stain
from some remote horizon banked with cloud;
as if light were green seed, and not bright shroud.

This morning yellow's green, and blue is green,
and brown and black and white and gray grow green.
This morning green is greener. Not a sound
except the threat of thunder, and the round
of water dripping leaf to leaf, from green
to green, from green to green to green to green.

(Petulu, Bali—1997)

64

Foreigner's Haircut

Placed on the garden path's uneven stones
the bamboo stool tips slightly to one side.
Close to my ear, I hear the squeaking tones
of scissor blades. Sometimes I catch the eyes
of several young boys seated at my feet
who stare in blank amazement, unabashed.
They know already that I sleep, and eat—
but here is evidence far more concrete,
more intimately human.
                             Shorn, unmasked,
I shower, check the mirror, step outside
to hang my towel in the sun. The last
few fallen locks of my own hair blow by—
re-animated by a passing breeze,
mixed with mimosa and hibiscus leaves.

(Petulu, Bali—1997)

All That Is Needed

For every lean brown cow, a makeshift shack for shelter
made of splintered planks and poles,
crowned with dented, rusted tin.

For every bamboo leaf, at dawn, one bead of dew,
crystal clear, and empty—open
like a lens to let light in.

For every petal floating on the surface of the pool,
shadows trembling on smooth stones
underneath still water's skin.

And for each wretch who falters, and falls beside the road,
an hour of sleep, and dreams—no matter
what he's done, or where he's been,

no matter where he says he goes,
or what on earth he thinks he knows.

(Petulu, Bali—2007)

At Web's End

The web has grown enormous overnight.
Last afternoon it bloomed in slanting light—
a boy's bright target for an idle man.

Unable to resist, I moved my hand
and little else from four to dark o'clock
until the sagging net was chock-a-block

with pits and peels and twigs—its spider rocked
and swayed on torn trapeze by each collision
of snare with bloodless prey. My inanition

acquired, as darkness fell, a strained precision.
Those things I could not reach for with my arm
were eye-grasped and, as mischief turned to calm,

to feed the central dead-eye of the storm
I tossed my loaded gaze into the maze
and furnished it with all that waning rays

of sunlight could supply. Thus ending days
grow empty as they dim—till shadows close
the spaces between things, and distance grows

beyond that point where measure knows
its place. Like when one wakes up dead.
All night, in dream I fear the web's been fed

what lies inside my eye. My eye's been bled.
How else explain the labyrinth's increase;
how my world shrinks as it grows more obese.

Its hunger for fresh tribute's my release
from my poor room which overnight's been morphed
into the weightless dollhouse of a dwarf

whose matchstick chairs and tables I toss off
this porch into the garden—where they're caught
like beads on sticky strings. Once I have brought

the last of my brief toys to its great naught,
the last remaining ounce of my own weight,
my teeth, my hair, my nails strung up like bait,

web-crowned at last—
                                        at last I'll abdicate.

(Petulu, Bali—1999)

A Dog Barks In It

A dog barks in a distance that is somehow farther
than the farthest clouds dispersing on the horizon.

Then suddenly the dead are whispering in my ear
of the long journey they've made.

Sometimes it is balled up here in my pocket.
Sometimes it dissolves just before dawn.

The herons are flying through it right now. And tomorrow
licking stamps at a post office—I'll be sending my letter off into it.

It's going nowhere, and it's never returning.
Or it's brought, like a wave, by deep water.

(Petulu, Bali—1997)

The Bright Stinking

The smoke of burning trash attends the dawn.
It billows from the gully down the road,
then rising, thins to stench—until redrawn
by sharply slanting sunlight's search for gold.
The night's last mists and morning's fouler smolder
now mingle to stern biblical effect—
each mote is gilded, haloed, each made bolder
by a ray of revelation's bright prospect.

And yet the brutal angle of this light,
its luminous geometry, sets free
a gentler stream of paler, purer white
ascending from my cup of cooling tea—
whose rising strand of steam's the secret leaven
in this stinking smoky sunlight sent from heaven.

(Petulu, Bali—1999)

70

Cloud Watch

Most afternoons, the heavy rains here keep me
half-willing prisoner upon my porch—
immobilized without, and yet completely
at sea within—assailed by that strange force,
that vehement activity which fills
a restless man the moment he's been stilled.

Though chained to my chair, becalmed by violent weather,
within this head that's cradled in my palm
transparent thoughts collide, condense, and gather
in passive parallel to outward storm—
whose driving wind and rain can scarcely vie
with gusts and squalls unleashed behind my eye.

The monsters children find and quickly lose
in skyscapes roiled and furling overhead
are no more and yet no less real than those
invisibly fermenting in my head:
those thoughts embodied, soon dissolved; that clot
and crumble of what is and yet is not.

Yet by dusk—exhausted thunderheads are drained,
dispersed by brutal blasts reduced to breezes.
The inner wrack that courses through my brain
has likewise thinned until its trace of steam is
more gently discharged, cirrus-like, uncoiling,
set free from water that's no longer boiling.

Bright vapor drifts across the moon. Stop talking—
I tell myself. Stop thinking. Go out walking.

(Petulu, Bali—1998)

Jacaranda

I'd been here once before: on this dry red road
dividing bustling town from fallow field—
a mute frontier beyond which overflowed
the contours of the yet-to-be revealed.
A sign, hand-lettered, stopped me in my tracks
(its language one I could not understand).
I stood and stared with longing. Then turned back,
and thought—I'm still a stranger in this land—.
But now I have returned. Three years have flown
yet little's changed—. Still walking, still alone.
The dust raised by my feet is still deep red.
The warning sign still stands. The road's deserted.
And magnetized by distance, I still clearly see
that long twin row of purple flowering trees.

This time I do not hesitate. I stride
across that threshold, down that narrow lane,
past trunks lined up like sentries on each side.
Above—below—the same pale purple stain:
a froth of blossom hanging like bruised cloud
from branches interlocking overhead
reflects the fallen petals that enshroud
the ground beneath my feet. Straight up ahead,
one low red hill—. Beyond, a patch of pine—.
The trees have thinned, and as the purple tide
recedes, I turn just once—fanned out behind
like peacock's tail or like ship's wake I find
my path comes to a point, sharp as a knife.
I climb the hill, convinced I've changed my life.

(Pyin Oo Lwin, Myanmar—2007)

– 4 –

NO MAN

Already

How old is my ghost? How old is my ghost?
                                    —*Peter Redgrove*

I'm leaving here tomorrow—and already
(untroubled by this human weather passing)
I hear the garden growing on behind me;

the pond disturbed, but only by the eddy
of circling fish—a slight, bright splashing.
I'm leaving here tomorrow—and already

such casual music can't help but remind me
how little of myself I leave that's lasting
in this garden I feel growing on behind me.

An unseen wind is rising, growing steady,
while overhead dark, gentle clouds are massing.
I'm leaving here tomorrow. Look! Already

rain's ready to erase (so none can find me)
all trace of tracks upon the ground. I'm asking:
in this garden I feel growing on behind me

how many times have rain and wind refined these
melting backward glances, this light grasping?
I'm leaving here tomorrow—and already
I hear this garden growing on behind me.

(Petulu, Bali—1997)

Invitation

Patience will help
To save, but will not come unless invited.
—E. A. Robinson

Though through the fingers of your hand
I flow like water, pour like sand—
Though early be devoured by late,
Yet leave me time enough to wait.

Explode your seedling. Split your bran.
Strip what you weave from naked man.
Let light from darkness separate.
Yet leave me time enough to wait.

I'll care no more for truth than lies
When I am meat for future flies.
Let patience hollow out from fate
No more, no less, than time to wait.

Reduce the mansions of creation
To one deserted railway station.
Let empty track be my estate,
And leave me there—with time to wait.

No Man

"My name is no man."
(Odysseus, to the Cyclops)

I

'All upright things are bent and bowed by wind…'

All upright things are bent and bowed by wind.
Who taught your hair to argue with the wind?

Be still now. Let this rose collapse.
Why whisper in an overwhelming wind?

Here is the place we built, and here we knelt
till storms arrived to simplify with wind.

Each breath I draw now is a corner turned
too suddenly, face first, to meet warm wind.

How long can one frail singer's voice pretend
that anyone can rearrange the wind?

Each night the tops of trees begin again
the task of ending somewhere in the wind.

Here is no man. He slips right through your arms.
He can't control the volume of the wind.

II

'I enter, hesitate—then turn my back…'

I enter, hesitate—then turn my back.
What will be done I'll do behind my back.

Through all the gaps and corners in spilled milk
I feel the lash of moonlight on my back.

From outside looking in, pale curtains drawn,
there is no arm or hand, no breast, no back.

I'm not the same. Where are the trees, the grass?
A field of darkness can hold nothing back.

Lock the door, my love. With star-crossed arms
I'll reach, in strained embrace, around my back.

The moonlight on the river runs away.
Don't take, don't take—it sings—don't take me back.

No man's lips are moving in the dark.
Which lover sleeps? Who feels the moon, bareback?

III

'In the hand that always waits I hold a glass...'

In the hand that always waits I hold a glass.
Wine's supple ruby rim defines the glass.

Face to face with distance at the window,
my mirror bleeds into a looking glass.

I've read the lines that cross our palms. They're cracks
within the curve of smooth stained scarlet glass.

Arrival I have learnt by now is loss—
your hips, transparent, shattering like glass.

My wine and I agree: this moonlit fog
is breathing's mark upon a sky of glass.

Pass slowly through my dreams tonight. Be gentle.
Tonight my bed is spread with sheets of glass.

Eye's heavy lid—. No man. Impatience lost.
A red moon barely rises through the glass.

IV

'I'm staring at the stars. I cannot sleep...'

I'm staring at the stars. I cannot sleep.
Sheer numberlessness will not let me sleep.

Saints kneel at night, poor men lie counting sheep,
while witches meet to peel the dark from sleep.

What filled the night before there were these stars?
What needle pricked these perfect holes in sleep?

Bowed heads, dropped lids—sink down! Now multiply
like ripples through the deepest rings of sleep!

At night the dead collide with drunken men
who gather round to guess the weight of sleep.

What can a creature tossed by time expect
from the immobile second hand of sleep?

No man who sings his own frail lullaby
will ever hear the other half of sleep.

V

'*Ten thousand seeds are scattered through the world…*'

Ten thousand seeds are scattered through the world
by every breath or breeze that stirs the world.

With every oyster and a single pearl,
come, let us play this shell game with the world.

No series of swift steps I take can bring
me nearer to—or farther from—the world.

Engraved on ancient maps, in ink that fades,
are waves beneath which shipwreck claimed the world.

Will ordinary skeletons and brine
be all receding tides tell of our world?

A light, like dust, from brutish darkness hurled.
A drone of stars. A honeycomb. A world.

From destined distance will no man return?
Is there a way on earth to end the world?

VI

'Hidden cards gripped tightly in one hand…'

Hidden cards gripped tightly in one hand,
coin counted—. Then the voice: "Let's see your hand."

I fell on stones so often as a child,
I learned how breath cools scraped and burning hands.

I've read the news. I'm traveling on the train.
I cannot keep from folding up my hands.

In a dry-ice crystal ball, through burlap drapes
my fate and I are stumbling hand in hand.

Now clenched, now unclenched, clenched, unclenched again—.
Then the dove, released, from the magician's hand.

I kneel at water's edge to see whose face?
I stoop to sip cold water from whose hand?

To be emptied of reflection; to embrace no man;
to break the handle from the cup; to unhand.

VII

'A pocket with a hole may give you nothing...'

A pocket with a hole may give you nothing:
a feminine hashish, an airy nothing.

By traveling circus moon tonight, come quickly—
bring wheel of light, bring lash—and spare me nothing!

Marooned gold garnishes the heads and hips
of stripped and shaven slaves. They bear me nothing.

The past is like a tune I hum myself.
You ask what came of all my fury? Nothing.

The stilled hands of stilled men still gather dew.
Now rest in peace—because we bury nothing.

A puff of seed, a flush of cling, my dearest.
Again—four aces and unwearied nothing.

There is a path that leaves no man behind—
where no one's learning how to carry nothing.

The Mandarin Orange Tree

Like water traveling through an unseen silk
its odor captures all the threads of space,
re-weaving them until each fiber's filled
with what remains when color's been erased.

Or might it be one drop of silk that stains
a water's depths, an ocean in the air?
Now water's silk! Silk's water! —Still unchanged:
this smooth continuous perfume everywhere.

Beneath the tree's dark foliage there pause
two men conversing of events in time,
of sweat and strain, of stern unbending laws,
laws lost within this unseen cloud's sweet rhyme,

this orange silk adrift, this orange sea
where boundaries between garments melt and blend
and swooning, vanish into fragrance. See—?
Where one begins the other never ends.

(Pujung, Bali—1991)

OTHER BOOKS BY DOS MADRES PRESS

Jennifer Arin - *Ways We Hold* (2012)

Michael Autrey - *From The Genre Of Silence* (2008)

Paul Bray - *Things Past and Things to Come* (2006), *Terrible Woods* (2008)

Jon Curley - *New Shadows* (2009)

Deborah Diemont - *The Wanderer* (2009)

Joseph Donahue - *The Copper Scroll* (2007)

Annie Finch - *Home Birth* (2004)

Norman Finkelstein - *An Assembly* (2004), *Scribe* (2009)

Gerry Grubbs - *Still Life* (2005), *Girls in Bright Dresses Dancing* (2010)

Richard Hague - *Burst, Poems Quickly* (2004)

Pauletta Hansel - *First Person* (2007), *What I Did There* (2011)

Michael Heller - *A Look at the Door with the Hinges Off* (2006),
    Earth and Cave (2006)

Michael Henson - *The Tao of Longing & The Body Geographic* (2010)

W. Nick Hill - *And We'd Understand Crows Laughing* (2012)

Eric Hoffman - *Life At Braintree* (2008), *The American Eye* (2011)

James Hogan - *Rue St. Jacques* (2005)

Keith Holyoak - *My Minotaur* (2010)

David M. Katz - *Claims of Home* (2011)

Burt Kimmelman - *There Are Words* (2007), *The Way We Live* (2011)

Richard Luftig - *Off The Map* (2006)

Austin MacRae - *The Organ Builder* (2012)

J. Morris - *The Musician, Approaching Sleep* (2006)

Rick Mullin - *Soutine* (2012)

Robert Murphy - *Not For You Alone* (2004), *Life in the Ordovician* (2007)

Peter O'Leary - *A Mystical Theology of the Limbic Fissure* (2005)

Bea Opengart - *In The Land* (2011)

David A. Petreman - *Candlelight in Quintero - bilingual edition* (2011)

Paul Pines - *Reflections in a Smoking Mirror* (2011)

David Schloss - *Behind the Eyes* (2005)

William Schickel - *What A Woman* (2007)

Lianne Spidel & Anne Loveland - *Pairings* (2012)

R. Nemo Hill is the author, in collaboration with painter Jeanne Hedstrom, of an illustrated novel organized according to the processes of medieval alchemy, *Pilgrim's Feather* (Quantuck Lane Press, 2002), a narrative poem based upon a short story by H.P. Lovecraft, *The Strange Music of Erich Zann* (Hippocampus Press, 2004), and a chapbook, *Prolegomena To An Essay On Satire* (Modern Metrics, 2006). Editor of EXOT BOOKS, www.exottreasures.com/exotbooks, he lives in New York City, but has for over twenty years traveled frequently to Southeast Asia. His travel blog, *ELSEWHERE*, can be accessed at www.rnemohill.typepad.com.